Joyful
sorrowful, glorious
reflections on
life and the rosary

Father Mieczyslaw Malinski
Translated by Reverend Walter J. Ziemba
Illustrated by Andre Chappaz

Credits: design—Glenn Heinlein; all artwork—Andre Chappaz.

ISBN: 0–89570–160–X

First Printing, February 1979

Claretian Publications

Joyful, sorrowful, glorious reflections on life and the rosary

Reverend Mieczyslaw Malinski

PART I

The Joyful Mysteries

1. THE ANNUNCIATION

The Annunciation.
The call. Vocation summons.
  To work. To action. To silence. To prayer.
The call. Vocation summons . . . to a confrontation.
To a friendly handshake. To a smile. To a kind word.
To resistance. To protest. To sacrifice. To dedication.
An invitation to something that tests your endurance
       that exceeds
         your self-imposed limits.
Limits which your fears have imposed upon you:
     fear of obstacles
     fear of losing what you have amassed
        what you have earned
        what you have acquired
        what you have come
         to own
        what you have grown
         accustomed to
        what your laziness has
         inflicted upon you
         your aversion to
         any effort
         any hardship.

The Annunciation.
Your eyes open to what you have not seen
               though you've passed it a thousand times.
Your ears open to what you have listened to so often
               but have never heard.
Your heart becomes sensitive to what is happening around you
               which before was never your concern
                                    never interested you.
But this is only an offer . . . summons.
You can say no.
You can refuse to hear
               to notice.
You can turn your head the other way
               out of laziness
                    looking for comfort
               out of habit.
You can make excuses:
                         you don't have time
                         just don't have time.
          Too bad it didn't come sooner
                    or won't come later
                    really, some other time would be better
                              in different circumstances
                              under different conditions
                              at a more propitious time.
Then . . . you'd be willing.
          But . . . not now . . . you can't be bothered.
          You're all set
          you're all ready . . . for something else.
And besides . . . you can't leave everything you have
you have to stick with the sure thing.
You can't take blind risks . . . wild gambles
so . . . you ought to stay where you are
                         where you can be sure
          what time is breakfast
                    lunch
                    cocktails
                    dinner

with whom you can have
        a pleasant and peaceful
                conversation
        shoot the breeze
        exchange juicy gossip
        share the latest rumors.

Maybe . . . some day
        you'll even decide to change all this—
            when you're bored with it all
            when your sources of income are cut off
            when it just doesn't pay anymore.
Right now . . . it doesn't look that way.
Right now . . . it's all peaches and cream.
And even if things changed
how can you be sure that to answer this call
is something you would like to do?
Good heavens, you were never called to heroic virtue!
        You never wanted to be here.
        Who needs monuments

either now
or after death?
Time flies . . . you'll probably stay anchored where you are
forever.
Though you have to admit
that sometimes . . . there's a hankering for the yonder
to take a chance
unfurl your sails
travel far away
while there's still time
to visit
unknown countries
seas
mountains
worlds.
Once more
to spring forth to God's call
while there's still time —
while there's still time
to accept the Annunciation.

2. THE VISITATION

A sense of obligation
a feeling of responsibility for someone
                              for something.
Because someone is waiting
              someone is counting on you
              someone is expecting help.

And even if he's not waiting for you
              if he's not counting on you
                      because he has no right to
                      and you're not obligated to him
                              in any way
              what if he does need help?

Obviously, you can reply that there are others
                              in his circle
              who are obligated to him
              who ought to help him.
He has his relatives
              friends
              those he has helped
              who owe him debts of gratitude.
They should assume responsibility for what's going to happen.
It will be a burden on their conscience
                              not yours.
It's none of your business.
              He has nothing to do with you
              shouldn't even interest you.
But . . . what if he really needs help
                      more and more?

You argue: helping would encourage the laziness
              of those who are responsible for him.
              That wouldn't be right
                              just.

That would be sticking your nose
in someone else's
business.
After all, you have enough of
your own problems
your own obligations.
They aren't easy to fulfill.
But . . . what if he has to go on waiting
for any kind of help whatsoever
and doesn't get it from anyone?
Remember . . . he's in need
alone
lonely.
He's in a tough situation.
Maybe he's not even looking for material help
just for someone
who is sympathetic.
Don't say your presence doesn't mean much
can't be of much use . . . because he's not your age
that there are two totally different worlds involved
two different generations
and you see no way in which you two could communicate.
For . . . you know
this is not a case where the alms of a smile
or a comforting word
or even a heart-to-heart talk
would be enough.
What is needed is more time for contact
for staying with him
for companionship.
The Visitation.

Because . . . in the end . . . it turns out
goodness transcends all differences
of age
and culture.

Finding a good low tar is tough.

You must simply go straight to the one in need.
Hear him out.
This is primary.
Let him talk . . . speak his mind
                    pour out the flood of grief
                                        bitterness
                                        sorrow
                                        misfortune
                                        depression
                                        indecision
                                        injuries
                                        injustices.

And you . . . listen.
Say nothing . . . keep quiet.
Don't interrupt.
Just listen.
Let him talk.
Maybe he doesn't even need your advice, your guidance.
Maybe it's enough for him just to talk to you
                    to you . . . a good person
                    who's ready to help him.

11

And then . . . when it's all over
you'll see for yourself
                his helplessness
                his mistaken vision of the world
                his erroneous opinions of people
                his unnecessary, overpowering fears
                        complexes
                        prejudices
                        grudges that have ruled him.
Maybe he'll admit all of this
                        even without your help.
You'll see . . . how little it took to have his life change
                                return to normal.
All it took . . . was patiently to untie the knots
                                unravel the snags
                                smooth the wrinkles
                                untangle the complications
                        enlighten what had become obscured.
Then . . . you'll see that it was really
                        much more complicated
                        than at first it seemed.
But . . . that it's not impossible to set right
                                to repair
                                to correct
                                to soothe
if only . . . someone would help
                if you would help
                just a little bit

                                of your Visitation.

3. THE NATIVITY

To be a mother.
For nine months . . . to carry a child within yourself
       to feel its first movements
       to share in the mystery
        of a person's coming into being.
       give birth
       hear the first cry of your child
       behold it
       cuddle it
       feed it with your own breast
        be nurse
         comforter
         slave
no longer to live for yourself
always . . . to be available
     at every beck and call
          when it cries
          when it smiles.

    To cuddle
     soothe
     hush
     sing lullabies.
    To cook
     wash clothes
     mend
     clean.
    To carry in your arms.
    To seek a hint of understanding on its face
       as you talk to it.
    To leap from your bed at night . . . strain to hear.
    To help with those first clumsy steps
   with those first efforts around the room.
  Feel the tight squeeze of its tiny hand
  hear spoken for the first time
    the most beautiful word in the world, "Mama"
    the first "What's that?"

the first "Why?"
    Tell stories
    explain
    instruct
    advise.
    Teach everything:
        to eat . . . to count . . . to read
        tie laces . . . wash hands
        brush teeth . . . keep order
        to play with other children.
        To be a dragon
            a wolf
            a bunny.
        To pretend crying . . . laughing
                indignation . . . anger.
To be a mother.
To feel that first withdrawing of a tiny hand from yours
   hear for the first time: "I'll do it by myself."
                "No, don't come with me."
                "I don't want you. Go away."
                "I'll manage without you."

"I know better than you."
"What do *you* know?"

To be a mother.
      Haven.
      Support.
      Protection.

        A refuge where one can grumble
                cry
                be calmed
                be soothed.
      Where one can be cheered
            affirmed in
                one's existence
                one's being.

To be a mother.
In time . . . to see your child leave
      walk into life's turmoil
      where one has to fight for every inch of ground
          for every piece of bread.
Finally, in the end . . . each time
      to wait longer
      to await her return
         her arrival
         late in the evening
         then . . . late into the night.
      To know deeper loneliness.
      To feel useless
         because she can manage alone
         because mother is unnecessary
         because your child has found new sources
            for happiness
            for help.
Now . . . only casual visits
      birthday greetings
      formal-sounding telephone calls
      dinners.
Because your child . . . now . . . is herself a mother.

Because . . . now . . . she has to be for her own children
> a strength
> a comfort
> a consolation
>> refuge
>> support
>> encouragement.

To be a mother.
> Remain alone.

Still, in spite of all
> you are the only one who knows what it means
> to be a mother.
> You alone . . . know how much this child is yours.
> You can prove it.

Only you . . . know how much that child took from you
> your thoughts
> your words
>> smiles
>> habits.

You never expected to hear your child repeat your opinions
> after so often rejecting them.

You see . . . how your child goes about life applying
> the principles you taught
> astonishingly, surprisingly.

You see . . . your life reflected and extended in your child.
> Amazingly . . . you verify: this is your labor
>> your creation
> which all began with your child's
>> Nativity.

4. THE PRESENTATION

The Presentation.
To trust in God . . . surrender yourself to him.
To fear not—
              neither present, nor past, nor future
to fear not for yourself
   fear not for those closest to you.
To trust in God who is your present
                              past
                              future.

         In whom you move
                     live
                     exist.
         He won't leave you
              won't forget you
              won't forsake you.
To trust in God, who is goodness
                     justice
                     honesty
                     law.
To trust . . . feel sure it's the only way to live.
To trust . . . to begin to live with God.
                     To live in justice
                              honesty
                              truth.
Ignore what's going on around you.
Ignore how other people act
      how they judge your actions.

To trust . . . to take heart
              to forget yourself
                   forget your fears of how you'll manage
                                   where you'll live.
              Because . . . fears lead only to that endless road
              always to want more
                              more money
                              more things.

To use your accumulated wealth
       your possessions
       as protection
       against misfortune
           poverty
           illness
           death.

To trust. Take heart . . . from your world
                  from those around you.
To enjoy life, people, the earth.
To delight in them
   get involved
   take the risk of such a life . . . trust people.
Not all of them are money-hungry
          covetous of titles and trinkets
          calculating merchants who count only
          what they will get out of it
          how much they will make.
People can be unselfish . . . sincere . . . open.
You can count on their help
       on their friendship.
You can have confidence in yourself
       that you're not such a coward
       that you really can do a lot
          more than you've done so far
       that you're not so out-of-joint
             burnt-out
             cynical
             decadent
       that you haven't as yet uttered
             your last word.
Trust. Seek out people, the world
   and not money, status, things, titles, honors.
   Don't always calculate how much you'll get
          for this or that—
          how much you'll earn

how much they'll pay you
for your smile
good word
graceful bow
gift
loan
help.
Rather . . . live for the Cause himself
the All.

Trust . . . that you can do some good.
Help when help is needed
lift when someone has fallen
lend to save what could be lost
smile to make others smile
not so you'll get something for it
but because you're supposed to do that.
You're supposed to live in justice
honesty
truth
God.

Open your eyes
and you'll see how many unresolved difficulties,
how many problems there are around you
in the area of your own interests
in the sphere of your own possibilities
in the context of your own talents
abilities.
That's the way to live.
And people will swarm around you like bees around honey
will encircle you to get a light from your fire
from your radiance.
You won't be lonely.
Trust . . . in people, the world,
yourself,
God.
Offer your life to God.

5. THE FINDING OF JESUS IN THE TEMPLE

Trying to find those lost years
        the lost road
        the meaning of life
             of another person.
Trying to find those years spent in ignorance
                in neglected opportunities.
Trying to find a way out of the maze of life
        answers in a labyrinth of questions.
Trying to find, day after day
        the wasted years
           people
           talents
           work.

Trying to find a friend
        someone who would want to be with you
           at least for a little while.
           To listen to you
              advise you
              guide you
              or at least smile at you.
Trying to find that friend
        among people who are absorbed
           with their own problems
           with their own private affairs.
Listening for a familiar voice
           close
           friendly
           cordial
           kind.

Waiting
     as one day drags after another
     with no hope that anything will change.
Looking for your lost road.
       For there was a time when you walked in the sun

                    you knew why you were living
                            why you were working.
            You had a lot of people around you
                            you had a friend.
And now
            you can't even explain to yourself
                    how you came to lose all of this.
                    Someplace you went wrong
                    stumbled into some kind of
                            mysterious labyrinth.
            You were deceived by some kind of illusions
                                    half-baked ideas
                                    half-truths.
It seemed to you
                    that you were discovering new worlds.
In reality . . . you were getting bogged down . . . mired
                            deeper
                            and deeper
only to discover, at last
                    with surprise
                    with astonishment
that you were empty-handed
that so many years had already passed
and you were still only a little past the starting-line
that you had wasted so much time in aimless wandering
that your colleagues
            your friends
            your contemporaries were successes,
                            had achieved something
            and you were actually just beginning
            at an age when all that
            should already be far behind you.

If only you could start life over again
            or at least push it back several years
            to correct your mistakes
            straighten your paths

salvage some of the hours spent on needless
talking
seeking
floundering.

And yet
constantly
it's the same streets
the same houses
the same people
with their plastic faces
the same smiles
the same "hellos" and "good-byes"
that say nothing
that mean nothing.

You're waiting for a change
a transformation
a renewal
a revelation.

In the meantime
day flows after day
month after month

and you begin to realize how dull you are getting
                        how there's less and less hope
                        for anything to change.
But . . . with what's left of your conscience
            you can't accept life as it is.
            With what's left of your human sensitivity
            you are convinced
            that you will not stay that way to the end
                        until you die
            that something will happen in your life
            that you're not finished yet
            that there is still an unrealized potential in you
                        a strength
                        which lies dormant
                        waiting for fulfillment.

And then
            it's like finding the evangelical drachma
            like seeing the biblical burning bush
            like hearing a choir of angels
            totally unexpected
            when all seemed lost
            when all hope had died
            when your patience was exhausted
to be found like a lost sheep
to embrace and listen to the heart beat with joy
to resolve . . . never again
                        at any cost
                        to wander away
                        with anyone
                        to anyone—
to follow only him
            who is the Truth
                        the Way
                        the Life . . . forever.
Because . . . once again you were found
                                    by him.

PART II

The Sorrowful Mysteries

1. THE AGONY IN THE GARDEN

A nagging premonition—something is wrong.
More than a premonition.
   You can already see . . . the black heavy clouds
          forming on the horizon.
   The first bolts of lightning
     claps of thunder from afar.
You lock yourself in your apartment
     draw the drapes
     put on the lights.
Wait out the storm, make believe you don't even know about it
         you haven't even noticed it
         it's not important.

But . . . you realize that this is even worse.
   It's lonely in your locked apartment.
   The streets are empty.
     Fear of the impending downpour
     has swept everyone from them.
   The late ones dart across the streets
       to reach home before the first drops fall.
No one will come to visit you.
    You hope longingly, secretly, to see a familiar form
         to hear the doorbell.
    Maybe one of your close friends will drop in
      his hidden fear camouflauged by a smile.

But . . . you know . . . you're kidding yourself.
                    There'll be no visitors tonight.
          Aren't the storm clouds gathering over you?
          Doesn't the storm hang right over your house?
                    You feel left alone, like a leper
                    abandoned by even your closest friends.
          Who wants to look at someone else's bad luck?
          They'd rather go home and mind their own business.
But . . . weren't you all in this whole thing together?
          Didn't you and they share in everything
                                        equally?
Yet . . . by some strange quirk
          you are left alone
          and they've sneaked off . . . behind your back.
Now. . .you'll catch the bolts of lightning
          and they'll just be passive observers
                of what's going to happen to you.
                Maybe . . . they'll even join the opposition.
That whole thing . . . it wasn't just your private business
                                your private affair.
It was all a matter of people . . . of better management
                    of prudent action in the name of Justice
                                for the Cause.
The Garden.
          You see what you have coming to you
                    for what you did.
                    You took the risk.
You exhausted the patience of those
                    who from their perches
                    watched what you were doing
who thought you were attacking them
                    trying to usurp all the power.
The Garden.
          Night
              fear
                    dread
                    anxiety
                          indecision
26
                          worry.

Maybe . . . if it were possible
     you'd prefer
          to recant all you said
          undo all that you did
          get out of this mess
          you got yourself into.
Maybe . . . you'd like to contradict your previous statements.
Maybe . . . there's still time.
     Try . . . maybe you can still get away with it.
     Go
       tonight
           secretly
              furtively
   to those who planned the attack on you
         who want their revenge.
     Apologize
          beg their forgiveness
            their pardon.
   Ask them to forget the whole thing.
Maybe . . . they'll have mercy on you
                   on your fear.

Promise them
          you'll recant all you've been teaching.
Explain to them
          you were interested in something else
          you were misunderstood
          everything is OK
          there's no problem of any kind of injustice.
          Everyone is happy
             satisfied.
          No one dreams of anything
               but . . . the status quo—
               to leave it all that way.
But
   do you really want to deny everything you preached?
          Your time in
             the Garden.

2. THE SCOURGING

Blow upon blow.
       You labor in vain.
       Your efforts are fruitless.
              Disastrous coincidences
              bad luck
              nothing but disappointments
                  letdowns
              especially with people
              you ask for help.
              They make excuses
              don't keep their word
              don't fulfill promises
              lie to your face.
     They pretend to be preoccupied
                 so worried
        want to be rid of you
        deceive themselves
        speak to you on the run
        have no time for you
              even to listen to you.
        Talk endlessly
            about how much work they have
              what they have to do
        suggest you come back later.
        They claim: it's really not up to them.
             Someone else
             takes care of that.
             And who is the one?
        They don't exactly know
        that's not their department.
You stand on rubber legs
        you're afraid you'll fall.
You want to keep your composure.
But . . . you feel your shoulders sagging
        your back hunching.
You try to maintain your natural smile

But . . . you know your eyes and cheeks are sinking.
Hot and cold flashes run through you.
You nod agreement.
You say, I understand.
That's the way it is.
Of course.
Definitely.
You feel sick.
You want to vomit.
With great difficulty
you force the words
just to say something
to retain some shred of your dignity.
You can't wait for this conversation to end
for this awful scourging to conclude.
With a superhuman effort
you manage what is politely called a smile.
But . . . you know it isn't.
It's only a skeleton's grin.
You're left alone
leaning against a wall
your head buzzing
completely emptied
like a helpless child
who doesn't know the way home.

29

For the umpteenth time
      even though you didn't want to believe it
      you convince yourself that you're lost
                  finished.
        Everyone avoids you.
That's the way it is
        encounter after encounter
        conversation after conversation
        friend after friend
        day after day.
            There's no end in sight.
The Scourging.
        Blow after blow falls upon you
            tied to the pillar of helplessness
            growing progressively weaker
            from pain
                despair
                revulsion
                disgust
                    with people
                      yourself
                  the fate prepared for you.
Scourging.
      They jostle you
        scorn you
        look at you disdainfully
        smile at you ironically.
            They are unhappy with you.
            They make no secret of it.
            They tell you to your face
                lecture you about it
                call your attention to it
                remind you of it
                warn you
                threaten
                chastise
                preach moralizing sermons.
This is worse than an argument

more humiliating than a public scolding.
They explain how you should behave
            what they expect of you.
Scourging.
            No one says a word about your accomplishments.
                        You have unquestionable merits.
                        Your intentions were the best.
                        You tried as hard as you could.
                        Their accusations are so unfair—
                                    gossip
                                    fairy tales
                                    backbiting.
            Maybe there is a sliver of truth
                        but not the way they're saying it.
            What they're saying is downright detraction
                                                wrong
                                                unjust.
Scourging.
            You remain silent.
            You know the one thing they're all waiting for
                        is for you to begin to defend yourself.
            You're silent.
            You know
                        this is the only way
                        to ransom the residue of your
                        humanity during this
                                    your Scourging.

3. CROWNING WITH THORNS

You stand . . . alone . . . before the mob.
They sit at well-provided tables
    tell their jokes
    laugh.
And you stand before them . . . alone
                exhausted
                friendless
                forlorn
                almost unnoticed.
    You gaze upon their contented expressions
            their fashionable clothes
            their sumptuous dining.
    You're not jealous
only . . . you have so many worries in your head
          so many anxieties
             unresolved problems
             uncertainties.
If they notice you
        it's only to make you
        the butt of their jokes.
        They laugh
            you're such an idealist
              so naive!

Aren't they right?
These men . . . who are discussing
        the special features on their new cars
        and who got what new job
        and what his salary and benefits are.
Aren't they right?
These women . . . who are always
        right up on the latest fashions
            and styles
        and who's having an affair with whom
        and who knows about it.

Aren't they right?
                How they exploited you
                by making you an expert on helping others!
As soon as they spot anyone who is in need, crippled, poor
                they send him to you.
                They assume the air of great benefactors
                as if they were doing you a big favor.
Maybe . . . if you weren't there
                if they didn't have you
                                they would begin to help.
                Of what use were your efforts
                                your endeavors to serve others?
How many times did it happen
                that these needy
                                wronged
                                helpless people
                just pulled your leg
                                used your hands
                to get their own chestnuts out of the fire?
They bothered you
        took up your time
        took advantage of you.
How much money did you lend?
                                You'll never see it again.
Then
        on the street they pretend
                        they don't see you.
Was your charity really necessary?
Were your way-past-midnight discussions of any value?
If you were to tally
                the hours spent in listening
                                talking
                                patching
                                mending
                                appeasing
                                soothing
                on settling their affairs for them,

                          doing their work
          they would run
                          not into days or weeks
                          but into many months
                                even . . . years.
The meaning of your life
the value of such a life.
                          You wonder.

          Did you really *help* those you were helping?
Really
          couldn't they have gotten along without your help?
          And . . . all you have is a bundle of letters
                    that some day
                               you'll have to discard
                    and some greeting cards
          that haven't been arriving too faithfully
                         in recent years.
Sometimes
          you even meet some of your charges
          those whose lives you have shaped
          and . . . according to your judgment
                    shaped definitively.
Truthfully . . . nothing has changed.
          They're still having their problems.
          Maybe different from the ones you handled.
          Maybe someone else is helping them now
          or . . . they're handling their own difficulties.
In any event
          they don't need you any more.
          Their chit-chats with you
                    are still personal and warm
                         but . . . somewhat detached.
          They even promise to pay a visit
                         to telephone
                         but . . . they never do.
          They never mention the money you lent them.

But . . . new people keep coming along
                                without letup.
    You listen to what they're saying
                to their complaints
                their problems.
    You try to find some kind of solution
                to invent some kind of resolution
                        that in their sorrow
                                and discouragement
                will give them a bit of optimism
                                        calm
                                        joy
                                        hope
which you . . . yourself . . . have long since lost.
    You explain . . . illustrate . . . beg.
    You can't take it . . . and you explode!
    They get on your nerves
                        but you fight not to get angry.
    Once again . . . you're filled with resentment.
    All you know is you're tired
                        weary
            that you've wasted a lot of precious time
                and . . . it seems . . . nothing will change.
You have so many of your own unresolved difficulties
                                and problems.
And no one is even interested enough to ask about you.
    Everyone presumes you're always doing fine.
    And really . . . there's not even enough time
                                for your own needs.

    You know
                it won't change
                people will always be coming to you
                and . . . you will try to help
                                to mend
                                to soothe
                                to cheer.

35

They'll force you.
They'll look to you as their comforter,
                      teacher,
                      adviser,
                      model.
You'll be their mainstay
desperately trying to solve their problems
           remove their troubles
without faith . . . in what you're doing.
Helping others
        even though you yourself need help.
Comforting others
        even though you yourself need comfort.
Leading others
        even though you yourself
        stand totally spent
            tied
                and crowned with thorns.

4. THE CARRYING OF THE CROSS

It's so tormenting
        painful
        every step an agonizing effort.
Can't fall.
     Must go on
          deliberately. . . step by step.
The gravel underfoot . . . so rough and sharp.
The cross on your shoulders . . . the crushing burden
          of your duties
          of daily, hopeless martyrdom.
          Like a yoked animal
              no freedom to choose
              no change in sight.
              That's your life.
              Everyday's story.
     The same daily routine at work
     the same daily routine at home
     preparing the meals, washing the dishes
     making the beds, cleaning the house
     dusting, storing, arranging
     shopping, picking up, exchanging
     miles and miles of hopeless daily traveling.
Thousands of details . . . trifles
       dumb nothings . . . that just get in the way
           take up your time.
Finally . . . you get to your real job
      a parody of anonymous service to your neighbor
              your country
              mankind
      which you can't even see through the stacks
         of papers, machines, trivia to attend to.

Yet, you're always expected to be calm, composed, collected.
   Is that what your life is supposed to look like?
   Is that what your love is supposed to look like?

Is your love to be so minutely fragmented
                    that it totally disappears?

Your Way of the Cross.
                    The irritating buzz of your alarm clock.
                    One dream, request, plea
                              from this prisoner
                              sentenced to hard labor—
                              to catch a few extra winks
to close your eyes just for a couple of minutes more
to forget for a moment what is waiting for you.
But . . . you know so well it can't be.
          You won't get this favor.
          The whip of duty flogs you painfully.
Unconsciously . . . you resist waking up
                              opening your eyes
                              standing up.
               You detest facing the new day
                    loathe the life that awaits you.
               You move like a sleep walker.
                    Thoughts move sluggishly.
               The disc jockey's time announcements
                    speed up your washing and dressing.
You hurry . . . almost panic that you may be late.
     Breakfast . . . you can't even taste it
                    it sticks in your throat.

     You shudder to think of the day you're about to begin
          leave your stuffy house
          only to plunge into the polluted air outside
                    into the rush and madness of cars
                              and people
                              all in a hurry.
          You still try to defend yourself
but . . . already . . . yesterday's unfinished business
                    preys upon your brain.
          You push it out . . . away

you have a right at least to a peaceful trip to work
but . . . already you're looking for answers
                                    solutions
                                    ways and means
                to resolve the problems
                        untangle the messes that have developed
                        for which there seem to be no answers.
            You still want to remain peaceful, quiet
but . . . in your mind . . . new ideas, expressions, phrases
                        press their presence.
            You see all the hustle and bustle around you
but . . . your thoughts are already on the job.

                The day gains momentum
                morning wakes in you
                                    you're alert
                                    sharp.
            Your first Good Mornings to your friends,
                    colleagues' first smiles.
            You get down to work.
            You surprise yourself:
                            whence all this optimism
                                    calm
                                    confidence
                        trust that all will go well?
In a couple of hours, though
                        you'll feel the wound in your side
                                    the trembling hands
                                    growing tension
                                    exasperation.
And . . . you'll see how tired you are.
                Then
                        a supreme effort to arrive at the moment
                        when the hands of the clock
                        end one more segment
                        of your
                                Way of the Cross.

5. THE CRUCIFIXION

Face it: you can't do anything any more
　　　　you can't go anywhere
　　　　you can't think about anything
　　　　　　　　you can only suffer
　　　　　　　　hands and feet nailed to the cross
　　　　　　　　a crown of thorns on your head
　　　　　　　　　　　sickness
　　　　　　　　　　　paralyzed hands and feet
　　　　　　　　　　　a splitting headache
　　　　　　　　　　　your consummate loneliness.
Cut off from the world around you by illness
you struggle for breath
　　　constantly uncomfortable
　　　　　　　　perspiring
　　　　　　　　clammy
　　　　　　　　disgusting to yourself.
You try to turn on your side.
There isn't a single painless spot on your whole body.
　　　　　　　　　　　Every bone
　　　　　　　　　　　every muscle
　　　　　　　　　　　everything hurts.

You can't sleep.
You can't think.
You can't stop thinking.
　　　Confused memories go through your head.
　　　Every noise
　　　　　　voice
　　　　　　melody
　　　　　　knock
　　　　　　hum
　　　　　　irritates you.
　　　Every detail that isn't exactly the way you want it
　　　every kindness and unkindness
　　　every visitor who comes and who does not come
　　　　　　　　　　　　annoys you.

You can't stand the people who mill around you
                 who take care of you
                 who are supposed to help you—
                 they all only irritate you.
More and more . . . you are convinced that they are
                 brutal and indifferent
                 rude
                 stubborn
                 mean
                 and thoroughly insensitive.
                 They have no idea how you are suffering.
Your friends who visit annoy you
because they come out of politeness
and look at you from the perspective of their own hardy health.
They sit in your room concerned only about themselves
                 hardly even notice you.
They behave so unceremoniously . . . never noticing
                     your suffering.

They begin with questions about your health
                 and how you feel.
But . . . it's clear that it's of no real interest to them
although some . . . with difficulty
                 try to comprehend
                 the meaning of their questions

and . . . maybe . . . even try to empathize
                    with your Lazarine condition
                    as with a beggar, lying at their feet.
But immediately they move on to their own affairs
                    tirelessly reel off their own problems
                    asking your advice, opinion, stand
                    begging for your help
                            your intervention
                    as if nothing in your life had changed
                    as if
                            you were the same person you were before.
You listen to it all . . . hardly believing your own ears.
You can't understand what these people want from you.
            Your head is splitting
            you're nauseated
            your throat is parched
            you can hardly see.
You try to mumble some word
            put together some kind of thought
            try to help in some way . . . just once more.
            At the same time
you see the mountain of unfinished work you have
            which you know won't get done by itself.
            You have to complete, settle, finish it.
But . . . you know it's too late for that.
            You just didn't have time
                    didn't get to it.
That which was to be the great work of your life—
            a life which was to be your great work—
now looks like a messy heap, a tangled web
            which no one will ever be able to organize and sort
                    put into separate files—
            if they can even find someone who would be interested
                            in doing it.
You just ran out of time.
You don't want to think about it now
even if it's just for a good cause.
You're just not interested.
42

All you want is to live
but . . . not at any price
       not at the price of pain.
All you want . . . is to be healthy again
            to go for a walk in the park
            listen to the birds sing
            sit by a stream
            swim in the ocean
            go skiing.
                  Not really "again"
                  because there never
                  was time in your life
                  for all of that.
Maybe . . . when you were young.
But . . . lately . . . you didn't even go for those walks
             or sit by the river
             or go to the shore in summer
             or the mountains in winter.
            There never was enough time.
            Always on the go.
            Just enough time for a little rest.
            And even then
            there was almost always someone else
                to look after and care for.
Of course, you always promised yourself there'd come a time
        some day
        when you'd find time for all that.
Now . . . you know it's beyond the realm of possibility.
Now . . . you'd only want not to suffer any more.
                To die.
                To die as quickly as possible.
       If only someone could render you that service
                do you that favor
                and end your life.
Now . . . you don't want to suffer so any more.
       You don't want to bear the agony of
                    your Crucifixion.

PART III

The Glorious Mysteries

1. THE RESURRECTION

They sealed your tomb with a boulder of slander and derision.
    Stationed a guard.
Announced pontifically that you were dead and buried
        your name would never again be mentioned.
They did you in . . . by force
           deceit
           avarice
           and a few pieces of silver.
      You were the loser.
They gave you a trial
    brought in a verdict
        and a sentence.
Then they executed you
        destroyed you
        stripped you of all your glory
                which you so deserved.
They pirated all you had accumulated
        with your life of hard work, heavy labor.
They fired you from your job
    removed you from the post you held
    took away your co-workers, colleagues, friends.

First, they labeled you a maverick
                    then an eccentric
          and, finally, a social misfit
                    teacher of false philosophies
                    threat to society.
          They turned your name into an insult.
          What a crime!
You were the only one who knew that you were right
                                        not they.
Maybe there were a few others who were convinced of that—
                    a few very close friends
                    and a couple of almost-strangers
                    who came on the scene
                    almost at the last moment
                    hoping to save you.

But . . . it was already too late.
                    Everything had been settled formally . . . legally
                                        according to their statutes.
You are the criminal.
Those who murdered you are innocent . . . before the law.
Society looks upon them as the champions of truth
                    protecting the common good
                    defending law and order.
Your tomb is sealed.
                    Silence
                    deafening silence
                    sepulchral indifference.

And yet . . . you arose from the dead.
                    Contrary to hope
                    despite presumptions
                        expectations
                        logic
                        forecasts
                        predictions
          you're alive . . . though they say you were buried.

You arose from the tomb of oblivion . . . infamy
                      contempt . . . and apathy.
You begin to appear among the people again.
    They speak of you with respect
                    admiration
                    praise.
    For the young
        you've become a hero of the struggle
                for truth and justice
                        unyielding
                        enduring
                        fruitful.
Your whole life's concern
              what you fought for
              what you repeated so often
                  is now on the lips of the people.
You yourself can't fathom how this got to them
              in what circumstances they accepted it
              how they were able to grasp it so profoundly.

Your Resurrection.
     And you thought . . . all your efforts with that fellow
                           you'd picked up along the road
                           like the Good Samaritan
                                       had been wasted.
   You thought he'd amount to nothing.
   You were sure there'd be no results.
   You were convinced you'd get no response from him.
Until . . . you hear the news
               see with your own eyes
               hear with your very own ears
               actually meet him . . . and verify:
                              this is a new man!
And he's so mature, prudent, sober in outlook
          so enthusiastic, involved, committed to the ideas
                      you once shared with him.
   You can't believe your own ears.
     What he's saying rings with what you once told him.
       No, doesn't "ring with"—
he's repeating you . . . almost word for word.
Weren't you convinced
          that you were pouring water into a sieve
          that it wasn't getting through to him
          that he was rejecting
          everything you were trying to tell him?
Your Resurrection.
               Your efforts were not in vain—
               your talking
                     explaining
                     challenging
                     serving
                     sacrificing.
               Ideas stick
               become incarnate
               take on flesh in people.
You've done well.
               Your enduring Resurrection.

2. THE ASCENSION

Your "Hello" and "Good-bye"; your "How are you?"
and "What's new?"
Your "Of course," and "Naturally," "Obviously,"
"Undoubtedly,"
"That's right!"
Your greeting, handshake, smile, farewell
your Christmas and birthday greetings
"All the best "
"Good Luck!"
You repeat the things you learned
assimilated
copied
looked up
were taught
what was pounded into you
what you were conditioned to do
reared to do
drilled to do.
The repetition of basic phrases, courtesies
and repetition of the biggest, most important words
touching the deepest roots
of your existence:
the meaning of life
love and death
truth and falsehood
justice and evil.

But . . . how much of all this is really your own, personal?
How much of the real essence of all this
were you able . . . on your own
to extract
accept
assimilate?
To what extent is this your own original thinking?
Do you know what you're saying?

Do you understand the words you utter
the objects you use
the groups you're involved in
and work with?

You act as if you were their author
and you're really only a nobody
not worthy to think, to express these words.
There's always that danger . . . that you'll be tempted
just to float through life
skimming the surface of reality
that you may race through life
knowing nothing about it
about people
about yourself
that you'll never discover who you really are.
And . . . here you are! All-important!
Your fate is at stake.
You've got to search for the meaning of life
basic values
fundamental truths.

The Ascension.
You are not the first. There were others like you before.
You are their successor, their heir
the next link in the phenomenon called humanity.
They all struggled with their weakness
with death
their sins

their longing for fame
and immortality.
Like you . . . they were tortured by monotony
frightened by the prospect of old age
saddened by the ephemeral.
There remained after them only fossils
cold lava
the dried leaves of their emotions
experiences
adventures
premonitions.
Bow before these human endeavors of words . . . things
institutions
before their works of poetry, prose, theatre
sculpture, architecture, painting.
Examine, listen, observe, enter into their spirit.
Through you . . . let them resound
with their former pain, love, joy, rapture
so that you could come alive, grow, awake, smile, bloom
so that dams could open in you
streams could tumble
seas could roll
stars could shine
heavens could open.
The Ascension.
For us . . . there remain
the fossils of the Gospels, sacraments, prayers
hymns, songs, antiphons, litanies, rites
devotions full of singing, playing, reciting
processions, candles, chalices
liturgical vestments, chasubles, albs.
For us . . . there remain
Christmas, Lent, Easter, Pentecost
the liturgical year
arranged according to the rhythm
of the revelation history
chapels, churches
decorated with banners

51

pictures, stuccos
plafonds, columns
friezes, architraves.
But . . . just so we don't get lost in all of this
let's remember
all of this came to be out of our great faith
in the meaning of human life
out of our love for him
whom we call the Beginning and the End
Truth and Justice
Beauty and Love
and you'll find that love in them.
But . . . because we're human
we're always in some sort of danger.
There are those who exaggerate
they so fall in love with the externals—
holidays, devotions, processions, prayers
that they can't go beyond them
they forget that these are to serve them
and are supposed to put love into life.
On the other hand
there are those who say the one essential thing is Love
so . . . who needs celebrations
private or public prayers
Mass, devotions?
That you can discard all this celebrating,
sometimes so boring and irritating to them.
Both extremes are equally dangerous.
Because . . . you celebrate to remember him
to be with him
to enter into his life
share his glory
to be his follower
in daily life
to be as open
free
magnanimous
as he who ascended into heaven.

3. THE DESCENT OF THE HOLY SPIRIT

These are the little qualms of conscience
                scruples that bother you . . . concerns.
These are your misgivings
                you feel like a scoundrel.
These are your self-accusations—
        that you've made yourself so comfortable
        that you're already so complacent, so content
        that you're so absorbed in amassing a fortune
            material objects, positions, honors
            citations, commendations, pomp, titles
            bows, greetings, compliments, signs of respect
            loyalties . . . fearful responses.

The Descent of the Holy Spirit.
    You hurt . . . because you hurt another.
    Your conscience pricks you
        for your dishonesty, abuses, shortcomings
        that unnecessary extra uncharitable word
        for ignoring the weaklings
        for your disdain
            callousness
            obstinacy
            stubbornness about trivialities
        just so you could show your superiority
                prove you're right
        for ridiculing those
        who might be in line for your job
        who are competing with you
        for the next promotion.

The Descent of the Holy Spirit.
    These are your little delights
                inner satisfactions
  which you feel when you've done something good—
        your enchantments, exhilarations
        bursts of strength and energy
        fresh ideas, new resolutions, new beginnings.

Suddenly . . . you open your eyes and see what was invisible:
new perspectives
new worlds
new possibilities.
You see a person you had never noticed before
even though he was always around you.
You listen to a person you had never understood before
even though she had always been talking to you
had always been asking you for something
always explaining something to you.
You notice your sorrow at someone's misfortune
your joy when someone receives good news
is successful
has good luck.

These are your words of praise to a stranger
                                  an acquaintance
                                  a friend
                                  a co-worker
                                  a rival.
This is your courage to tell the truth—
to say "Yes" when you're convinced you ought to say "Yes"
and to say "No" when you're convinced
                                  you ought to say "No."
This is your courage to put your trust in another person
                         believe what he says is the truth
                         support him to save him from others
                                                  and himself.

This is your new sensitivity
          to be able to feel what's going on in another person—
                         what he feels
                         what she's going through
                         what he's afraid of
                         what she needs
                         what he's dreaming
                         what will bring him a tiny bit of
                                            joy and happiness.
This is your new sensitivity
          to be able to appraise the values of your community
                                  your generation
                                  your people
                                  the world—
                                  its problems
                                     aches
                                     threats
                                     dangers
                                     tragedies
                                     directions
                                     tendencies
                                     developments
                                     trends.

To understand the concerns and the anxieties
                              that trouble mankind.
To face them squarely, seek answers
                    solutions
                    cures
                    preventives
                    medicines
                    help
                    salvation
              propose solutions
              get involved
              accept what's good
              reject what is wrong
                              false
                              pointless
              respond to the needs of the times
              build a new world
                    a better world
                       more beautiful
                       more glorious
                       full of Truth
                       Justice
                       Goodness.
Respond to

              the Descent of the Holy Spirit.

4. THE ASSUMPTION

No choice: you have to live here on earth
                              take life seriously
                and be involved in the matters of the world.
You have to get to work on time
        and cope with the problems that the day and life bring—
            listen to people and take them seriously
            share their problems and their joys.
You have to settle business
                        give speeches
                        affix seals
                        build, close, open
                        clean, eat, dress
                        provide for today, tomorrow, and after-tomorrow
                        care about clothes to wear
                                    a place to live
                                    something to eat.

But . . . remember . . . all of this is a bit unreal.
            Even when you're happiest
                when you're genuinely moved
                                        perturbed
                                        saddened
            it's still a little bit make-believe.
All that's happening around you
        that you're involved in . . . up to your ears
        none of that should be able to knock you off your feet.

The Assumption.
        Nothing on earth could drive you to absolute despair.
        Nothing could bring about an absolute tragedy.
        Nor could any one thing bring you absolute happiness.
                              There is no *absolute* loss
                                    no *absolute* gain.
        Nothing is permanent . . . immutable
                        except Goodness, except Love.

And . . . when you see people scurrying about
                              always in a hurry
          over-involved . . . over-worried
          taking life *absolutely* too seriously
you realize what a big mistake is their *absolutely*
          and their madness brings an indulgent smile
                              across your lips.
In a sense . . . you have to be detached in your life
                              from material things
                              from your money
                              from people in your life.

Because . . . everything is passing, ephemeral, temporary
          and . . . you're only a pilgrim
              with a long way to go
          a way you see more clearly as you grow older.
And . . . the older you get
          the stricter you must get in evaluating
                              those bygone years—
                    your immaturity
                    covetousness
                    greed
                    attachments
                    lack of poverty of spirit.
How much were you willing to give
                        share
                        donate
                        bestow
                        lend
                        pardon
                        forgive
                        forget?
              Did it come easily?
The more water over the dam
the more must you look to the road that remains before you
                    must look to your Assumption.

5. THE CORONATION

To fall in love, fall in love with someone, love something.
To go . . . beyond the hills
                    beyond the rivers
                                the forests
                                the seas.
To discover
                    a stream
                    a flower
                     bread
                    a treasure
                    a most beautiful pearl.
To fall in love.
                    Spellbound . . . swept off your feet.
                    Carried away. All agog.
                    Trusting. Full of hope.
                    To remain. To cling.
                    Be constant. Be faithful.
To fall in love.
                    Commit yourself. Become one.
                    Sacrifice. Surrender.
                    Spend hours upon hours
                            day after day
                            week after week
                            month after month.
        No sparing of self
        no sparing of time
        no sparing of money.
                            No accounting.
                            No calculating
                                how much will you earn
                                how much will you spend
                                how will you make out
                                    will it pay?
To fall in love.
                    They laugh at you, that you're naive

don't look after your business
you work for nothing
you're worth more
they're taking advantage of you.

But
   even if your love was not reciprocated
   even if your loved one abandoned you
                betrayed you
                disappointed you
                failed you
                lied about you
                cheated you
                took advantage of you
                violated a confidence—
  even if you parted
    if you had to leave
          separate
and . . . even if your work
             the labor of your life
             was taken away
             credit was given to someone else
             awards were conferred on those
             who had little or nothing to do with it—
   even if your work was destroyed
      its development or restoration impeded
don't conclude you lived in vain
          that you wasted those hours of elation
                     plodding
                     toil
       because nothing came of it.

Not true.
    Love is the only true value of life
          true meaning
      the only thing that remains.

Only with Love is there no chance for error
         disappointment
         disenchantment.
Really . . . those are the only years that were not wasted
      nor was your toil
      nor was your effort.
Because . . .
    Love is one
    just as Truth, Beauty, and Goodness are one
    as are service and dedication to them.
That's what really counts.
That's why you can't let them snatch Love from your grasp.

Because . . .
    then all you have left is self-concern
    pursuit of important positions
       honorary degrees

titles
awards
honors
citations
medals
generous honorariums
luxurious cars
summer cottages
plush apartments
art objects
overstuffed chairs
antiques
expensive paintings
rare crystal
the latest in refrigerators
newest in gadgets
automatic washing machines
giant-screen TVs
quadraphonic stereos
trips to romantic islands.
All you'll have left . . . is concern about yourself
your health
every stuffy nose
angina attack
sore throat
irregular heartbeat.
All you'll have . . . is checking your blood pressure
drinking herb teas
visiting health spas
searching for unusual health foods
going on fad diets
visiting quack doctors
faith healers.
Therefore
don't let them snatch your Love from your heart,
Because then
all you'll have left is your money
and money has an alluringly dangerous charm.

It promises everything.
First . . . you must amass a lot of it
                    as much as possible
                    by any and every means.

Then
        it tempts you with the illusion
                    that when you're very rich
                    you can really live!
        You can work, understand, love
                    dedicate yourself
                    be honest, decent
                    be happy and sad.
Then you can help other people.
        They will shower you with respect
                                    recognition
                                    esteem
                                    friendship
                                    and even love.

But remember
            when you fall prey to such a temptation
            you'll never again do anything else but
                        hoard money
                                    tirelessly
                    by every possible means.

And . . . you'll never have enough.
And . . .
     . . . you'll die.
And . . . you'll leave a lot of money.
And . . . on your deathbed you'll realize
                     you went through life
and . . . you don't know anything about it.
      You don't know what it means to live
      because you never learned what it means to love
         be happy
      because you don't know what it means to work
         to sacrifice yourself
         to be sad
         to be worried.
Only on your deathbed will you realize you wasted
                     your whole life.

Or . . . you won't realize *anything*
      because you'll be too far gone
      because your only goal in life was to
         preserve your own life
         live as long as possible
and that's not Love . . . it's only egotism.
That's not fascination . . . but only diabolical possession.
     It is not freedom . . . it is servitude
            it's hell on earth.

Because . . . there were only two options: Love
         or a trembling fear for your own existence.
One's freedom or slavery
      life or death.
            They begin here on earth
            as do happiness or misery
            heaven or hell.
     Which you choose . . . is up to you.
Life hereafter is a continuation of life on earth:
            it is its Coronation.